the KID WHO CLIMBED the TARZAN TREE

FLASHBACKS ON A LIFE SAVED BY A CHILDREN'S HOME

D.W. ROZELLE
AUTHOR

C.A. GROOMS
ILLUSTRATOR

C.A. Grooms assisted by nine-year-old Hanshan Wright-Miller

LITTLE CREEK PRESS®
A DIVISION OF KRISTIN MITCHELL DESIGN, LLC

Mineral Point, Wisconsin USA

Little Creek Press®
A Division of Kristin Mitchell Design, Inc
5341 Sunny Ridge Road
Mineral Point, Wisconsin 53565

Editor: Carl Stratman
Book Design and Project Coordination:
Little Creek Press

Second Edition
May 2016

Printed in Wisconsin, United States of America.

For more information or to order books:
www.littlecreekpress.com

Library of Congress Control Number: 2013950058

ISBN-10: 0989643158
ISBN-13: 978-0-9896431-5-3

Cover lithograph (1873) courtesy of the Waterford Public Library,
Waterford, Wisconsin. Steam lithographic printer, J. Knauber.
Contributor, E.M. Harney, et al.

DEDICATION

Alice Ann (Rozelle) Hough

1939-2010

For my late sister, Alice Ann, who suffered more,
forgave the most, and gave to her own children
a parent's love she herself had never known.

TABLE OF CONTENTS

PREFACE

ON July 6, 1944, at ages six and five respectively, David and Alice Rozelle were placed at Taylor Children's Home in Racine, Wisconsin. Their mother, Dorothy Rozelle, had contracted tuberculosis, necessitating her confinement in a Milwaukee-area sanitarium.

Initially the intent had been to return the children to their mother's care following her recovery. But following her release from Muirdale Sanitarium in 1945, Dorothy's predisposition to emotional instability, alcohol abuse and joblessness quickened. Her former husband, Chester Rozelle, had retreated from family involvement following the couple's divorce in 1941. By 1942 he had disappeared as a presence in the lives of his children.

As a result, Taylor Home became the Rozelle children's caretaker until September 1, 1949, when they were relocated to a foster home in rural Racine County, Wisconsin. This is David Rozelle's memoir of his nearly six years as "a kid from the Home." It is also his belated tribute to the progressive philosophy and humane staff of the now-vanished Taylor Children's Home.

The only reason for time is so that everything doesn't happen at once.

—Albert Einstein

GHOSTLY THRONGS

In which lost children, long dead,
play in the ruins of their Home.

Dedicated with ceremony in 1872, demolished with none in 1972, Taylor Orphan Asylum disappeared without a trace of historical reverence or regret. Its fate has become an all too familiar spectacle of our time: today's bulldozers wantonly pulverizing yesterday's progress.

So it was for this century-old progressive sanctuary for children. The reforms of its past were ground into the debris of our present—out of sight, out of mind and, ultimately, out of memory.

The history of Taylor Home—as those of us who lived there called it in the 1940s—cries out for its emulation, not liquidation. During its one hundred years of existence, the Home's principles and practices gave enlightened refuge to scores and scores of indigent boys and girls, among them the author of this book.

The building itself stood like a magical Arthurian fortress on acres of beautiful Wisconsin country-side just south of Racine, Wisconsin. Its yellow brick, neo-Gothic exterior climbed three stories high, tall arched windows casting huge swaths of natural light into over eighty rooms.

At the very least, Taylor Orphan Asylum deserved historic preservation as a monument to its selfless founders, Isaac and Emmerline Taylor. Thanks to the bold beneficence of this nineteenth century childless couple, hundreds of downtrodden children found validation in the home these two had endowed with not only their wealth but also the humane bylaws they prescribed as its talisman.

But there is no monument. There is only a vanishing vision to be conjured—a vision of ghostly throngs of boys and girls playing among broken bricks and shattered glass within rooms without walls or ceilings, deliverance or song. ◉

The history of Taylor Home—as those of us who lived there called it in the 1940s—cries out for its emulation, not liquidation.

TAYLOR ORPHAN ASYLUM

JULY 6, 1944

*In which my mouth drops at my
first sight of "the Home."*

O n that day, my first sight of it astonished me. Racine's busy
Taylor Avenue, a major thoroughfare, abruptly yielded to a road
flanked by country pathways leading to nowhere, as far as I could tell.

And immediately there it was, visible through the car window to my
left, set back to the east among aging oak trees—an ornate edifice of
Victorian architecture worthy of a prince and his Snow White. We
had crossed an invisible borderline dividing Racine's urban from

its pastoral, dividing my
present from my future.
There it was. Taylor Or-
phan Asylum.

Gargantuan, constructed
from pyramids of cream-
colored bricks, it sprawled in nineteenth century Baroque splendor.
It ascended three gracious Gothic stories with stately windows tall
and arched, a stained-glass chapel snug against its north walls, and
high, stone chimneys amidst pointed dormers rising from higgledy-
piggledy mansard roofs. Magnificent.

And in photograph and memory, it still strikes me as magnificent:
a rooted refuge fit for the happy childhoods denied to both 19th

century English orphan Isaac Taylor and his more illustrious contemporary in childhood deprivation, the author Charles Dickens.

It was to be my home for nearly six years. It was a sunny summer's morning, July 6, 1944.

. . . .

It was to be my home for nearly six years.
It was a sunny summer's morning, July 6, 1944.

. . . .

EMMERLINE AND ISAAC TAYLOR

*In which a Kentucky belle and her English orphan
husband imagine an asylum for luckless children.*

They had turned out in portrait, in their best attire, to welcome
me as, at six years of age, I stepped for the first time into the
grand reception hall of Taylor Children's Home. I undoubtedly gazed
upward in bewilderment at the stolid likenesses of these rosy-cheeked
personages, serenely attired in the black formal wear of their time.

The gazes of these two—Isaac and Emmerline Taylor, founders of Taylor Orphan Asylum—were decidedly not directed at me, but toward
each other. Their half-length portraits, painted in rich oils and framed
in gold, hung on opposite
walls, directly across from
each other in an entrance
hall that spoke silently of
their benevolence.

Isaac Taylor, born in 1810
in England's Yorkshire County, had known firsthand the plight of
children in hard times. Orphaned at an early age, he had been marked
by the harshness of a childhood in an English poorhouse. Released at
last at age eighteen he worked his way to America in 1828, making his
way to Cleveland, Ohio, where he first exhibited the unusual coupling
of a Midas touch with a heart of gold.

Taylor worked and scraped to buy a horse or two, and soon became a prospering livery keeper in Cleveland. In the meantime his heart had won the heart of young Emmerline Martin. They married in 1835.

The marriage produced children. But in an ironic reversal of the misfortune of Isaac's childhood, the Taylor children died before their parents.

In 1842—undoubtedly sensing opportunity and perhaps in flight from the pain of the death of their children—they moved to Racine, Wisconsin, a small but growing port city on the western shore of Lake Michigan. There, Emmerline set up household, while Isaac headed north along the lake to Manitowoc County, where he invested in pine lands, saw mills, and real estate before returning to Racine. Midas had become a Wisconsin lumber baron.

The fortune which the threadbare Yorkshire orphan amassed in America was enormous for its time. His and his wife's worth at the time of his death amounted to half a million dollars.

During the short months before Isaac Taylor's death, with the knowledge that both he and Emmerline were gravely ill, they discussed the disposition of their wealth.

Isaac died in 1865. During the few months remaining in her life, Emmerline formulated a will that embodied her late husband's desire to found an orphanage. Emmerline died in 1866. The Taylor's left no heirs apparent.

"Apparent" now, however—one hundred and fifty years after their deaths—is that the beneficiaries of the Taylor's last will and testament were multitudes of children in the direst straits. I am one. We are the heirs of Emmerline and Isaac Taylor, founders of Taylor Orphan Asylum. ✿

....

Apparent now, one hundred and fifty years after their deaths,
is that the beneficiaries of the Taylor's last will and testament
were multitudes of children in the direst straits.

....

SWAMI CROSSFIELD'S CRYSTAL BALL

In which the new boy cranks up Spike Jones on the Victrola.

Take a moment. Imagine this, as I am years later. It's July 6, 1944, my first day at Taylor Children's Home. I am six, anxiously sitting on a small iron bedstead I've been assigned to the small, second-story dormitory called the "B-Boys Department." Like all the beds in the room, mine is painted chalk white, its  mattress covered by a heavy black wool blanket. My life, however, doesn't feel black-and-white to me. I fear I've been abandoned forever to the cavernous netherworld of a bad dream.

A short, middle-aged woman enters the room, distinguishable by a brown, four-buckle leather brace she wears on her right wrist. "Welcome, David." Smiling warmly, she takes me softly by the hand, leading me down a narrow back stairway and over gleaming hardwood floors into a high-ceiling library just off the grand entrance hall. Its shelves are lined with more books than I've ever seen. We take seats across from each other at a long, narrow wooden table. My legs swing nervously, like the pendulums in a crazed grandfather clock. She sits contentedly, as tranquil as an hourglass.

A crystal ball rests between us.

Miss Crossfield [smiling]: *David, we're very happy to have you with us. I am Miss Crossfield. I've printed my name on this paper for you. How do you do?*

David [to himself]: *Do I tell a lie? Do I say, "Fine"? I'm scared stiff. Where's my tricycle? What have they done with my bike?*

....

And, by the way, David, you may use the Victrola over there.
Music matters here. Humor as well. Have you heard Spike Jones's
latest, "Der Fuhrer's Face"?

....

Miss Crossfield: *I'm the person who'll be in charge of some of the fun things you'll be doing here, David. You'll be seeing quite a lot of me during the next six years.*

David [to himself]: *The next SIX years! Mom said a few months. How does this "Crossfield" know it'll be SIX years? What is she? A swami?*

Miss Crossfield [resting her hands atop the crystal ball, then closing her eyes tightly]: *Let's see what's in store for you at your new home until September of 1949.*

David [to himself]: *1949! She's goofy. That's forever! I gotta find my tricycle.*

Miss Crossfield: *Oh, I see lots of fun here, David. Lots! So much that I'll have to list them for you. Do you mind if I list them, David?*

David [shrugging his shoulders, then to himself]: *Why not? Maybe she'll mention playing that old record player over there in the corner.*

Miss Crossfield (looking at David): *Oh, I see so much for you over the years. In winter you'll be using pieces of balsa wood and colored paper to build model airplanes at this very table and kites to fly in the skies behind the Home in spring. We'll also make plaster objects to give as gifts to others. Oh, and during your summers, I see you and the other boys, on your own, riding a city bus to Washington Park pool. One day you'll be a good enough swimmer to do cannonballs off the highest diving board.*

David [growing excited and to himself]: *Me? I can't even swim yet!*

Miss Crossfield [Looking up at David and then down to her crystal ball again]: *I'll bet you wonder how you'll learn to swim. Well, every summer you'll spent two weeks in a big tent with your friends at a boys' camp called Camp Anokijig [an-oh-kee-gee]. It's in the woods and on a lake far from Racine. You'll be taught to swim there and that's not all. You'll ride horses, paddle canoes, learn to make your own bow and arrows, sing songs around a campfire every night, and, did I mention, play real-life adventure games in the woods? There's even, I'm told, a tiny cannon that's fired at sundown every night as the flag is lowered.*

David: [growing more excited but still to himself]: *A cannon! A real cannon! Geez! Maybe I'll get to play with matches.*

Miss Crossfield [sighing]: *And can you believe it, David? Back here at the Home, we're going to make puppets and give puppet shows. We're going to have talent shows, too, and you and your little sister will sing "Oh, Susanna" together at one of them. Later, you'll have the stage to yourself to sing "Tommy Toodles"—at far too high a pitch, I might add, so that your veins pop out on your reddened face. But that's OK. We'll laugh with you, not at you, as we always do here.*

And speaking of shows, we'll all watch movies together from the Home's grand staircase. Some of our movies will star Sunset Carson, Laurel and Hardy, Dale and Roy Rogers, the Marx Brothers, the Three Stooges, and even Lash LaRue, the King of the Bull Whip, though we don't believe in whips around here. "Better to laugh than to lash," we say.

David [eyes wide now, to himself]: *Hey, maybe when the movie's over they'll let me slide down those big banisters I saw on the staircase.*

Miss Crossfield: *Later, David, we'll have a look at the area behind the home. I see you'll be using the monkey bars, the giant sand box, the swings, the teeter-totter, the baseball diamond, the farm sheds, and the little pot holes you'll dig for playing marbles. In fact, you'll paint a picture of boys playing marbles that will be chosen for showing at a Racine art museum.*

You'll also clamp on roller skates to roll along our sidewalks, learn to ride a bicycle round and round our driveway, and practice throwing a football the right way, thanks to that nice Buck Kneister. Buck's a young man we've hired part-time so that there's a male around for you boys to talk to. Whew, David! I'm nearly out of breath.

David [to himself in amazement]: *Me, too! Forget the tricycle! I'm going to learn to ride a real bike.*

Miss Crossfield [especially attentive to her crystal ball]: *And best of all, David, you are going to learn to love to read. Why, you might ask, is that "best of all"? You'll understand in a few years. The books on these library shelves are yours to read. I will read aloud to you and the other boys. People will give you books to keep while you're with us. For the rest of your life, you'll keep them on your own bookshelves—Gulliver's Travels, Robinson Crusoe, The Last of the Mohicans, The Three Musketeers.*

David: [mouth agape, barely able to sit, but still silent]: *I've heard of all those guys!*

Miss Crossfield: *And, by the way, David, you may use the Victrola in the corner over there... and the radio, too. Music matters a lot to us here. Humor, as well. In fact, the record now sitting on the turntable is by Spike Jones and the City Slickers. Have you heard Spike's latest, "Der Fuhrer's Face"? It's one of his funniest. We've been singing it lately as we goose-step around this very table with two fingers held, like mustaches, under our noses.*

David [for the first time aloud]: *Gee, thanks, Miss* [reading her name] *Crossfield. I just knew I'd like it here. May I play the Victrola... right now?*

Miss Crossfield: *You may, David. And as we listen, you and I—if you like—can sing and march and laugh around the table together.* ◉

THEIR WILL IS THE WAY

In which a last will gives women the last word.

Orphans have long memories. All his life, Isaac Taylor had harbored, for good reason, bitterness against the males who had staffed the Yorkshire poor house of his boyhood. The proof lies in his will.

His wife Emmerline—who died within a year of Isaac in 1866—spent the dwindling months of her life drafting a last will and testament in accordance with her husband's deathbed wishes. We can surmise that these were her wishes as well. Isaac Taylor and Emmerline Martin had loved each other long and well.

Made childless by the deaths of their own children, the Taylors in their last months looked to the welfare of other children of other parents broken by hardship.

Their will earmarked a huge sum of money for its time ($185,000) to establish and endow an orphan asylum in the city they had adopted as their home, Racine, Wisconsin. $60,000 of that total enabled the will's trustees to purchase forty acres of idyllic rural land southwest of the city for the construction of a gigantic building.

No less than Lucas Bradley, an eminent architect and builder of the era, won the commission to design and construct the project. In addition, a permanent endowment of $125,000 was set aside to cover yearly expenses.

Not a bad outcome for a once penniless orphan, I'd say. But there was more to the will than money. There was extraordinary wisdom. The Taylors had thought it through.

First, their bequest provided that there should be "no political or religious test" for admission to the home. That, alone, illustrates the exceptional progressivism of the Home's nineteenth century founders.

But just as exceptional—and, in my opinion, even more striking—is this provision in the will: "There shall be a board of directors consisting of nine persons, five of whom shall be of the female sex, and four of the male sex." The orphan boy Isaac Taylor's memory of mistreatment by men had found expression in his will.

I have now had over half a century to reflect upon my experience as one of Taylor Orphan Asylum's offspring. My life has been, by and large, a happy one, marked by attainments and satisfactions that no one might have predicted, given my unpromising beginnings.

In the end, I attribute much of what I am to the foresight of the Taylors, who gave to women the authority—the last word, in effect— over the sheltering and upbringing of children lost to the world outside the Home.

During my time there, the Home thrived in the hands of good-hearted women: some of advanced, some of middling, some of ordinary education. What does it matter? What matters is that during every moment of my life with them, they held that I, like all children, was a human being in the making.

Thanks to these women and the will of my Home's founders, I "made it," along with many others. The credit is largely theirs. The rest belongs to more than a few precious persons in my life and to the mystery of being born human enough, as Isaac Taylor understood, to overcome a perilous beginning if given the chance. ◎

"There shall be a board of directors consisting of nine persons, five of whom shall be of the female sex, and four of the male sex."

TILL HE COMES
MARCHING HOME

In which a former "kid from the Home"
returns for lunch as a hero.

I entered Taylor Children's Home at age six during the momentous summer of 1944. World War II would rage on in Europe and the South Pacific for another 15 months. D-Day in '44 and the Battle of

Iwo Jima in 1945 would be etched onto historical memory in blood.

As I remember it, however, the war and its aftermath had little to do with everyday reality for us, except as a backdrop for romantic notions of warfare played out in imaginary games at the Home and in war-fevered Hollywood movies playing at downtown Racine theaters.

John Wayne as Lt. Cmdr. "Wedge" Donovan in The Fighting Seabees (1944) inspired many a bloodless act of roaring heroism on our playing fields and in the weeds surrounding the Tarzan Tree. Fix bayonets! (wooden snow-fence staves). Charge! (as in run and slash with your staves). To this day, the astringent scent of disturbed burdock catapults me back into ill-tempered patches of this burr-bearing weed. In summer it lay massed beyond the tamed landscape far to the rear of the Home, as if in wait for our war games.

We also sang the popular songs of the World War II era. I can still sing sizable chunks of the now obscure "Johnny Got a Zero" (a tune about a boy who scored 'zeroes' in the classroom, then later, as a young fighter pilot, shot down a Japanese fighter plane, a "Zero").

But there were also periodic reminders by adults that our country had called upon us to sacrifice, a word we dimly equated with patrio-

I still harbor the memory of one WWII veteran, a young man in a dress brown uniform. He had returned for a visit—a boy from the Home.

tism. Wedge Donovan, for instance, had put his life on the line for our America and, not surprisingly, for his co-star in "The Fighting Seabees," the glamorous Susan Hayward.

And so we happily participated in "paper drives" by pulling coaster wagons from house to house to collect newspapers and magazines for recycling in the war effort. And we donated a tiny portion of our tiny weekly allowances to purchase wartime savings stamps. Later I cashed in my stamps to buy a small camera. (See "Baby Brownie? Baby Ruth"?)

During the war's aftermath, we ate every last Brussels sprout on our plates in deference, as we were told, to "poor children in Europe and Japan who had nothing to eat." As it turned out, they didn't have much to eat, while we kids from the Home had plenty. We learned early that deprivation is relative.

And speaking of World War II's end, would you like to see my Lone Ranger Atom Bomb Ring? Never mind. It went missing long ago. With fifteen cents and a Kix cereal box top, I sent for one in 1947. Advertised as "a seething scientific creation," one could, the ad promised, actually see "atoms" through the ring's small plastic lens. In what strikes me now as perverse, the ring also served to celebrate the use of science to end the war by immolating much of the innocent citizenry of both Hiroshima and Nagasaki. Safe in America, we kids at the Home really had no idea that war could be hell in places with strange names.

After more than half a century, I still harbor the memory of one real combatant, a young man in a dress brown Army uniform who one day sat during dinner at the Home's head table with our superintendent, Miss Roskilly. Either on furlough or mustered out, he had returned for a visit—a boy from the Home.

I don't remember what he said when he rose to speak to us. The picture in my memory frames him against the backdrop of a hand-painted mural on the wall behind his and Miss Roskilly's table. It had been there for years as far as I knew. Had that young soldier not visited us on that day I probably would never have remembered it.

The mural depicted, as I recall, robins sheltered among the green leaves of a peaceful tree, perhaps an apple tree. In a jiving tune recorded by the Andrew Sisters during World War II, a soldier writes a letter to his girl, asking that she be true till he comes "marching home."

Nobody sang "Don't Sit Under the Apple Tree" out loud that afternoon, though it plays loud in my recollection of the soldier who came home to "the Home" from a war "over there"—way, way over there. ✲

THE TARZAN TREE

*In which a muscular oak gives birth
to a chest-pounding anthem.*

We called it the Tarzan Tree. It stood alone, blackened by age, tough as time to the east, well beyond our playing fields. A gnarly, ancient oak, long-rooted among tall grasses and weeds, the

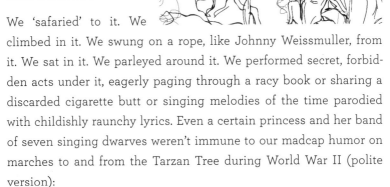

Tarzan Tree became a destination which provided privacy for our imaginations and forays into adult words and habits.

We 'safaried' to it. We climbed in it. We swung on a rope, like Johnny Weissmuller, from it. We sat in it. We parleyed around it. We performed secret, forbidden acts under it, eagerly paging through a racy book or sharing a discarded cigarette butt or singing melodies of the time parodied with childishly raunchy lyrics. Even a certain princess and her band of seven singing dwarves weren't immune to our madcap humor on marches to and from the Tarzan Tree during World War II (polite version):

Whistle while you sweat,
Hitler is upset.
Herman Goering dropped a herring,
In his bassinet.

Unquestionably our caretakers at Taylor Children's Home knew about CSTT, the Clandestine Society of the Tarzan Tree. The tree stood as a distant landmark, starkly visible from the Home's east windows. For all I know, these cheerful ladies called it the "Cheetah Tree," in playful reference to the "chimps" who played in it.

Nevertheless, our overseers never interfered with our secret lives under the Tarzan Tree, except to ring the brass bell that hung outside the kitchen to call us to meals. In return, as if by tacit agreement, we headed to the dining room, thumping our chests helter-skelter while yodeling Tarzan's triumphant yell: *Mmmmm-ann-gann-niii!* *Mmmmm-ann-gann-niii!* Call it our anthem. ◎

Unquestionably our caretakers at the Home knew about "CSTT,"
the Clandestine Society of the Tarzan Tree.

OUT ON A LEDGE

In which some daring-do fails to bring my mother back.

At about age seven, perhaps on two or more occasions, I perched on the third-story ledge of Taylor Home and threatened suicide. To my embarrassment it always came to nothing. The last time I threatened to jump not a soul screamed, "Oh, my God. Help! David's going to jump!"

As a result, within minutes I crawled back through the open window to resume forever a fulsome life off the ledge. My career as a child extortionist had ended. "My mother or my life!" lacked leverage.

A series of disappointments had led me to the ledge. Early on, after her release from a tuberculosis sanatorium, my mother would occasionally visit my sister and me. Usually the visits would occur on a Sunday.

She'd arrive from Milwaukee, dressed to the nines, gather us up, and then escort us downtown by bus or taxi for a stop at the zoo or a movie theater, followed by an interlude at a lunch counter. After a few hours she'd return us to the Home, sop up our tears with her hankie, kiss us goodbye and then dissolve into her other life.

I loved my mom, sometimes to distraction. A social worker's confidential report from that period notes that, "David worries about his

mother." It is no exaggeration to declare that this small boy wanted—sometimes desperately—to save his mother from the big, bad world she lived in without him.

As a result when she'd visit us and soon after leave us, I'd sometimes panic. Never one to suffer high anxiety without acting against it, I'd sometimes go out on high ledge to "ransom" her back.

My modus operandi was straightforward: I'd crawl out unto a third-story brick ledge from a window in the Little Boys Department and make my demands by yelling something like, "I'm gonna jump! Bring back my mom or I'll kill myself!"

The first episode may have set off alarms among supervisors, so I probably got sweet-talked—maybe even jerked—back into the room. But after a few of these empty jump-threats, they'd wised up.

Eventually they may have simply poked their heads out the window to inform me that the hand bells were about to ring for dinner and that I surely didn't want to miss dessert. They had obviously come to recognize my unfolding lust for life, including desserts. La dolce vita, David! La dolce vita!

Give these women credit. They were both wise and imaginative. They might also have sensed how damned scary it was to look down from that ledge upon racks of donated bicycles poised to impale me if I took the leap.

In my memory, I can still see those riderless bikes parked side by side as if to escort me by solemn procession to a cemetery. "Poor kid," mourners would say as the casket, adorned with a mangled Schwinn, rolled past weeping throngs lining the boulevards of Racine. "What a shame! The little orphan so loved his mother that he killed himself for her."

....

The last time I threatened to jump not a soul screamed, "Oh, my God! David's going to jump!" My career as a child extortionist had ended.

....

Incidentally, I don't recall ever being late for any Sunday dinner at the Home. Better on Sunday to eat dinner with your friends than to sprawl lifeless among the twisted spokes of broken bicycles.

Besides, my hot-wired, mentally ill mom had better things to do with her weekend nights than to soothe her tearful daughter and son. But that's no matter now. I've come to accept that my mother really and truly couldn't help herself. Life had broken her. But not me, not yet. ○

THE CANNED POTATO SALAD CAPER
A One-Act, One-Minute Play

*In which a scheming gang of small boys
buys a pack of Camels.*

The scene: *Racine, Wisconsin, circa 1948. A mom-and-pop grocery store on the northwest corner of Durand and Taylor Avenues, two blocks north of Taylor Children's Home. Four boys, about ten years of age, lounge outside against one of the store's windowless old brick sidewalls, talking quietly but excitedly. One boy enters the store, heads down one of its narrow corridors and stops at the canned goods, peering hard as if looking for something in particular. After a few minutes, the store's owner, in white grocer's apron, pencil behind ear, approaches the boy.*

Shopkeeper: *May I help you, young fella?*

Boy (blushing, obviously shy): *Ma sent me to pick up a can of potato salad. I can't find one.*

Shopkeeper: *Hmm. Let's see [glancing at the shelves]. Tell your mom I'm sorry, kid. Looks as if we're out of canned spuds. Did she want anything else?*

Boy [without hesitation]: *Yeah, a pack of Camels!*

We'd done it. Pooled our nickels and bought the real thing for twenty cents: a shiny, fragrant, unopened pack of fresh cigarettes! No more scouring of sidewalks for castaway, thumb-length, lip-stained, dry butts. Now, back to the Tarzan Tree, boys, for a real smoke! Zip-a-dee-doo-dah! ◉

We had done it. Pooled our nickels and bought the real thing for twenty cents: a shiny, fragrant, unopened pack of fresh cigarettes!

ALAS, POOR DURWOOD

*In which a good boy learns he's too bloody
good for his own bloody good.*

Ah, Durwood. I remember you well. Durwood. Alas, poor you. The darling of the Home's supervisors. The wunderkind of Mitchell Elementary School, in spite of your origin at the Home. The kid who owned a violin. Too often, I hated you.

So, probably, did my pal in all things great and small, Jack "Rosie" Roseberry. (In return, Jack labeled me "Daisy"). "Rosie" later became an outstanding athlete, albeit never a golfer as far as I know. More on golf later.

Nevertheless, it should be noted that we both grudgingly sympathized with you, Durwood. You were grievously prone to blood-awful accidents. (Is it possible that a predilection for spilling your own gore explains your coddling by motherly women?)

At any rate, I personally witnessed two of your most noteworthy mishaps. One involved a moving car, the other a golf club in motion.

The auto accident consisted of one hitting you as you walked home after school. I came upon the scene shortly afterward. People and parked cars were gathered around someone spread-eagled—breathing but prone as road kill—on Taylor Avenue. It was you.

You, Durwood, apparently had been walking home on the wrong side of Taylor Avenue, the side without a sidewalk, and a car struck you. Later, as I recall, we learned your leg had been broken. Poor Durwood!

The golf club accident took place months later, in the gravel play area directly behind the Home. One of us had laid hands on a golf club, iron, and a group of us were practicing our "swings" by teeing-up round pebbles on flat pebbles. That's when the inevitable Durwoodian bloodshed occurred. You stepped into someone's backswing, opening a gushing crimson hole in your forehead. Yes, you went prone again (as you had on Taylor Avenue) and attracted again (as you had on Taylor Avenue) a small crowd of hand-wringing gawkers.

I recall towels being carefully wound about your head by cooing supervisors. When they finished, you looked like Durwood of Arabia swathed in your massive, gory turban. I don't recall if you were transported to hospital by camel or ambulance but off you went (again).

In truth, Durwood, looking back at it all, I envied you. All of us at the Home, boys and girls, longed for the love and admiration of anybody—most especially the adults who ministered to us in loco parentis. You, bleeding Durwood, sometimes appeared to have won the lion's share of the affection we so coveted.

Forgive us, old friend. Although we may, for an instant now and then, have wished you harm, we never really did you any. Honest. Besides, in between your bloodlettings, there were songs to be sung and laughs to be laughed together, prone but unscathed under the spreading Tarzan Tree. ◉

You, Durwood, were grievously prone to blood-awful accidents.

ANNA AND BERTHA

*In which a mysterious pair of laundresses
toil and sweat and get crabby.*

Did we kids from the Home wear uniforms? Well, sort of, but we'd have had to strip down to our underwear, *en masse*, to prove it. Every kid, as far as I knew, wore what we called "Snuggies": machine-knitted, one-piece, knee-length, short-sleeved, button-up (including the rear) union suits.

Boys wore white. Girls wore pink. How do I know? From an attic ventilation grate in the floor above the Big Girl's Department, I once got a

look at Francine T. prancing in hers. She never knew.

Because all of us changed clothes at least once a week, we must have been

issued two sets by our dorm supervisors, who, poor women, had to laboriously ink, by hand, our initials on the inside collars. But two other employees had it worse. Imagine—if you dare—the heaps of ripening children's underwear that confronted our laundresses, Anna and Bertha, each week.

Every day, to and from meals, we passed Anna and Bertha's brightly lit downstairs washroom, its doors wide-open to the low-ceiling corridor that led to the ground-level dining hall. Massive, stern women, they labored mightily in steam and heat among noisy, giant machines, ankles deep in the soiled clothing of those urchins from upstairs. We never heard them complain.

Week upon week this stoical pair sorted our sordid laundry into piles and then heaved each load into a monstrous washer that churned and gurgled the dirt away. The next steps weren't any easier.

Drying the clothes first required cautiously feeding sodden laundry, piece by drowned piece, into a factory strength wringer. Watch your fingers, Bertha! Flattened but still wet, the lifeless clothing got pitched into a heavy metal tumbler for drying. "Ironing" followed, if needed, which entailed feeding wrinkled pieces into the jaws of a "mangle" for pressing on heated rollers. Unfolded, our clean bed sheets smelled of our laundresses' "cologne"—a blend of singed cotton and bleach.

Imagine—if you dare—the heaps of ripening children's underwear that each week confronted our laundresses, Anna and Bertha.

Finally, clean or else, Anna and Bertha folded and stacked each piece by department for distribution upstairs. These were proud working women. Who could blame them for beaming a bit as—red in the face, huffing and puffing—they hand-delivered the fruits of their labor?

Delivery, in and of itself, could have been no easy task for these aging, adipose ladies of the laundry. The Home stretched upward three stories, its 80 rooms connected by a labyrinth of twisting, sometimes claustrophobic, stairways.

Scattered throughout were various "departments," including five dormitories divided by gender and age, a large kitchen and dining area, staff living quarters, office facilities, maintenance and furnace rooms in the deep recesses of the basement, recreation areas, and a gigantic, unfinished attic whose bare, wooden rafters rose dizzyingly skyward. There was even a chapel (see "Next Door Magi"). Apparent to me now is that six years was not nearly enough for me to explore the Home's every nook and cranny, basement room and attic height, loosened brick and locked closet.

Anna and Bertha also took upon themselves the role of spontaneous hall monitors. My sister, for instance, was once ordered to kneel for a time in a corner of the laundry room. She'd been nabbed by one of them for running in the corridor.

Badly frightened, Alice never forgot the experience. All those machines. Those two hulking, laboring ladies. Would they ever let her out? Alice's fearful dark eyes, punctuated with an immutable frown, had been her birthright, plaguing her spirit until her death a few years ago.

My sister's terrifying beginnings had cursed her for a lifetime. Parents matter. Hers did, too, but as the agents of her inherent insecurity. Sixteen months younger than I, Alice had been positioned as a helpless infant to suffer the worst of our mother and father's insufferable faults. Her remarkable bravery, in concert with her determination to be a better person than her parents were, is now the birthright of her five grown children.

During my six years at Taylor Children's Home, Alice's punishment-by-kneeling was the only time I recall caretakers crossing the Home's humane line of discipline. That one single "infraction" aside, Anna and Bertha did, nevertheless, possess virtues worthy of our emulation.

In those days, many of us learned to work by watching grown-ups work. It occurs to me that Anna and Bertha—at work, in full view, "on stage" so to speak—served to dramatize the inevitable toil that awaited most of us as adults. Exemplary matrons of Wisconsin's work ethic, they suffused us with it.

Anna and Bertha illustrated the self-discipline that might, if we paid attention, make a respectable life for us as adults. The virtue of a lifetime partnership and laboring side by side would not be self-evident to children from broken families. Though we never took notes in the doorway to their laundry, we noticed as we hurried by.

When the day was done, Anna and Bertha crossed the gloomy passageway from their workplace to their shared apartment. No one I knew ever entered there. No one I knew ever knew anything more about them.

They didn't appear to be sisters or cousins or strangers who'd met on a train. Who were they? They were Anna and Bertha, Taylor Home's mysterious laundresses. Sternly energetic? Yes. Admirably hardworking? For sure. But in contrast, because we were children, we preferred to spend our energy having fun. In those days we took the sunny side of the passageway. ◎

UNDERWEAR BASKETBALL

*In which an unraveling union suit
unravels my athletic debut.*

One year Mitchell Elementary School organized a basketball game for the upper-grade boys against another school. I made the team. A kid from Taylor Children's Home had been tapped for athletic stardom!

The results of long but happy hours of practicing alone in a cavernous room in the lower depths of the Home had caught the eye of a teacher on the playground. This kid can run! This kid can dribble! This puny kid has a two-hand push-shot that bangs the rim now and then.

But my Taylor Home underwear spoiled it all. Although I had no "jock strap," I had no concern as I suited up for the big game: I figured my knee-length union suit could function nicely as my "jock."

Unfortunately, Mitchell's green shorts proved shorter than Taylor Home's underwear. But again, I figured "no problem"—I'll just roll up the legs of my union suit under my uniform shorts and play on to fame, fortune and the envy of the Big Boys' Department.

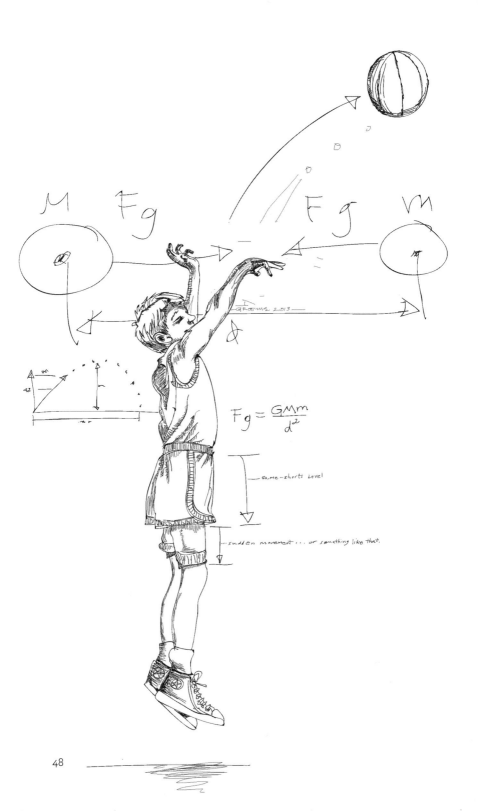

$$F_g = \frac{GMm}{d^2}$$

Game-shorts Level

...sudden movement ... or something like that.

What I didn't foresee, of course, was the impact of a fundamental law of Newtonian physics—gravity.

To my horror, as I ran up and down the court, the rolled-up legs cascaded below the level of my game-shorts. I nearly unraveled in embarrassment. Up and down the court, I desperately tried to hike up, roll up and even hold up with one hand my unfurling union suit.

My debut as a basketball star turned into frantic frustration—even disgrace. Mitchell's proud, playing- field green had become my glowing red-in-the-face ignominy. Among other humiliations, I'd let down the honor of Taylor Children's Home.

But then whose idea had it been to issue us weird undies with flaps in the back, buttons from top to bottom, and legs longer than basketball shorts? Not mine. To this day I stride the world in jockey shorts. ◉

I didn't foresee the impact of a fundamental law of Newtonian physics—gravity. Up and down the court I desperately tried to hold up my unfurling union suit.

WORMS

In which cheap, fresh fishing worms
may not be worth the wait.

The worms crawl in
The worms crawl out,
The worms play pinochle
On your snout.

—children's song

Big money was to be made at Taylor Home, relatively speaking. "Big" if you didn't have any beforehand (we didn't) and your wants were, like mine, lean. How "lean"?

On weekends I could take a bus from the last stop on Racine's south side (Taylor and Durand Avenues) to and from downtown Racine for six cents, round-trip. The four downtown movie theaters—the Rialto, Venetian, Badger and Main Street—charged fourteen cents for a child's admission to a matinee, sometimes a double feature. Treats came to another five cents. Grand total? Twenty-five cents.

So, for a quarter a day on both Saturdays and Sundays I could see two to four movies, treat myself to a couple of boxes of Milk Duds and pay

for two round-trip bus rides. Grand total? A half-dollar—that is, if I could earn fifty-cents by the weekend.

And I often did, especially during my last four years at the Home, when I was chosen to handle the "dirty-dish cart" after meals. That meant bringing the cart to each table at the tail end of meals in the dining room, having the kids (still seated) ceremoniously pass the dishware and utensils to me for stacking in the cart, and then running the full cart back through the swinging door into the steaming kitchen to be unloaded.

Don't feel sorry for me. The dishes I gathered up were all but "licked clean." The etiquette of the dinner table required us to "cleanup" our plates. There were no exceptions, even for glutinously creamed, salt-stricken chipped-beef on dry toast. None of us dared insult the cooks by so much as wrinkling our noses at the food they'd prepared for us.

My wages came to fifty cents per week, every week of the year. No wonder I couldn't wait for the weekends. No wonder I developed a love for cinema that's endured a lifetime. No wonder I still love bus rides, theater tickets and Milk Duds. I could afford them all.

There were, however, other ways to earn a little spending money at the Home. Nailed to a tree at the avenue's edge in front of the Home was a weathered, plain wooden sign painted by hand in crude red letters. It read, "WORMS 5¢."

On a charitable impulse, a driver (usually a fisherman), having spotted the sign, would pull into the circular driveway surrounding the Home and park his car. After some looking about, he'd stumble across an adult and ask, "How do I buy your five-cent worms? That's a nickel a dozen, right?"

....

Yet many of our warm-hearted worm buyers waited. Never has a nickel can of fishing worms cost so much in a buyer's wasted time.

....

The adult would ask him to wait while she rounded up "some of the boys." His wait often turned into a long one. Eventually boys would be found and dispatched with spades and tin cans to dig the worms from a field. They'd then return for the sale, if the customer hadn't lost patience and decided to fish "wormlessly."

And yet, many of our warm-hearted worm buyers waited. Never has a can of a dozen fishing worms cost so much in a buyer's wasted time than those sold by Taylor Home.

But worms or no worms, all of us earned a weekly allowance at Taylor Children's Home: five cents for the youngest, ten for the next oldest and so on, up to perhaps twenty-five cents.

During my first years the superintendent at that time, Hattie D. Mills, would solemnly award our allowances after lunch on Saturday. Mrs. Mills would rise majestically at her table and call us up, one at time, to hand us a little brown, sealed envelope with our name written on it. Each envelope contained the shiny coin of our allowance. "Thank you, Mrs. Mills," we'd murmur, and we meant it.

I started at a nickel, graduated to a dime, and then got promoted to the dirty-dish cart. A magnanimous fifty cents became my wage. My weekend afternoons at the movies had been secured.

There was, I'm sure, more to this business of allowances than I'd thought. Work was equally shared at the Home. Both boys and girls pitched in to sweep, mop and buff floors; to dust, make our beds, and clean bathrooms; to rake, cut grass, garden, etc.

A fair share of the Home's menial, yet substantial house- and grounds-keeping chores fell to us. None of this work, however, seemed arduous. None felt inflicted. No one denied us free time. There were, of course, scores of us to divide the labor among, and no whips, chains, bullhorns or stopwatches to keep us going.

I now believe that one of the purposes of the weekly allowance was to reward each of us for meeting the individual obligations of living life together in a single "household." Once, during the early years of my adult work-life, a colleague asked me if I had been raised in a kibbutz. I had no idea. "What's a kibbutz"? I asked. Once she'd explained, I thanked her aloud for the compliment.

I also silently gave thanks to Taylor Children's Home for creating the "kibbutz" I had lived in. Our chapel was not a synagogue, but our lives in many other ways were blessedly "kibbutzian."

BABY BROWNIE?
BABY RUTH?

In which I buy a camera to take photos I can't afford.

It's

still in my possession,

my first little big-time purchase,

saved up from weekly wages of 50 cents

schlepping dishes from dining room to kitchen.

Taylor Children's Home.

You heard that right,

Taylor Home,

Racine.

Me: *I want it, Mister,*

The camera in your shop window.

Him: *Baby Brownies don't grow on trees, kid.*

How's about buying a five-cent Baby Ruth instead?

Him again: *Here's how it goes, boy,*

"If you ain't got the

do-re-mi"

and so on.

I bought it anyway, kept it, too.

The shop and its keeper are long gone.

Nothing much in black-and-white survives a childhood,

Except maybe banged up Baby Brownie Specials.

What is it I once hoped

might come to light

in darker rooms?

Author's Note: The joy of using my Brownie was soon replaced by the joy of the possession of it only. I couldn't afford film or processing. Incidentally, a version of this work was read at Paoli House Gallery in October 2009 during a reception for the American photographer Pedro E. Guerrero. We Baby Brownie photographers stick together. ◎

Nothing much in black-and-white survives a childhood,
except maybe banged-up Baby Brownie Specials.

HELL HOLE SUNDAYS

In which a maddened mom calls heaven "hell"
and beats it out the door.

Late on Sunday afternoons, a pall stalked the Home. That was when those parents or other relatives with time and means would return their children to 3131 Taylor Avenue after a weekend or day away. The gloom was palpable. For both the parents and their children, parting was not always "sweet sorrow."

My sister and I were not often among the Home's weekend absentees. Our mom had other fish to fry, either waiting on tables or making whoopee. But for more than a few children, the weekend meant they'd be in for some face-to-face time with mom or dad or kindly aunts and uncles. I recall two incidents involving parents that reflect Sunday's gloom: one a somber tableau, the other a shrieking exit.

The tableau remains as vivid as a painting in my memory. As I walked by a dorm room on a late Sunday evening, I glimpsed a father sitting on the edge of a bed where his son lay, tucked in. The yellow bedside lamp at that moment softly spotlighted the pair. I sensed the boy's sorrow as the father tried to console him with his hands and words. I didn't stop. I walked on. Instinctively, we always walked on as parents and children succumbed to long goodbyes.

The second Sunday incident turned heads because it turned out to be theatrical, in stark contrast to the propriety which typically accompanied our evening meals. Taylor Home's dining area was located on the ground floor, between a huge kitchen on one end and a food storage room wall and entrance on the other.

We ate communally in assigned chairs, a supervisor seated at the head of each table of ten. Tables were arranged in two rows with a corridor in between for meal deliveries from the kitchen on one end and the general entrance on the other.

Painted in glossy pale-green enamel, the dining room's furniture gave off an orderly—even formal—appearance in keeping with the etiquette practiced throughout our meals. We did not sit until the supervisor sat and the same blessedly short prayer was recited in unison beforehand ("Bless us, oh Lord, and these thy gifts... ").

Here's how it went: Napkins on laps. Dishes of food passed and self-served. Forks or spoons in the right hand, knives in the left. Backs straight. Elbows off the table. Conversation subdued, punctuated, when appropriate, with "please" and "thank you." And at meal's end, "May I be excused, Mrs. Sorenson?"

One Sunday evening, from across the corridor dividing the table rows, I noticed a mother occupying a seat at a table with her child. That, in itself, did not strike me as unusual. Welcomed on Sundays to join their children for supper, parents sometimes ate with us, although not many took up the offer.

But this one had. A scrawny, bird-like woman with dark hair, she had caught my notice—perhaps only because of her appearance. More likely, because I sensed trouble brewing. Even now, my "skin" remains thinly attuned to tumult within others. Like a tamed coyote, I still

....

Sure enough. Midway through the meal trouble erupted.
The woman suddenly leaped up, her chair screeching backward.

....

count on "early-warning" intuitions to trigger my behavior. (See "A Streetcar Named Delirium.")

Sure enough. Midway through the meal trouble erupted. The woman suddenly leaped up, her chair screeching backward. "I'm getting out of this hell hole!" she screamed. In a flash she was gone, out the doorway. The dining room fell silent.

But not for long. Within seconds we had resumed eating. My guess is that no one's peas, including her daughter's, had spilled off the plate or that anyone skipped dessert that evening..

I realize now that this woman couldn't repel the mushrooming tension of having to leave her child. For a few moments an embarrassed hush had collapsed over the dining room. The daughter may well have collapsed later saying "Goodbye, Mom" to her pillow and praying to a god left speechless.

In the moments after the outburst, I might have whispered to the kid sitting next to me, "What hell hole does she mean?" My guess is he shrugged his shoulders, as if to say, "Beats me." And so we all ate on, not missing a forkful.

Years later I came to grasp the significance these two Sunday afternoon incidents. When parents showed up, so did distress. And when parents departed, so did distress.

What we thrived on were the consolation of regularity, the security of predictability and the numbing of woeful memories by these two certainties. Taylor Home provided them. Manners, too.

And speaking of etiquette, oh, how I wish that I had blocked that woman in flight with the following rejoinder, spoken in my best parody of the finest tearoom English: *"I beg your pardon, madam. This institution, I assure you, is not—as you have described it—a 'hell hole.' We, in fact, choose to describe it not as a 'hole' but as our HOME!"* ◉

TRAINS, TAXIS, CHINS UP

*In which my little sister and I tip our hats,
then tip the taxi driver.*

Now and then Alice and I found ourselves transported from the Home to Milwaukee for a weekend with our mother. As I recall, the Home's indefatigable social work supervisor, Mildred Wright, drove us there. It was up to our mom to get us back.

I've come to realize that our visits were infrequent for at least two reasons: one being that she preferred high times with adult males over downtimes with two little kids; the other, that she seldom had lodgings to host us in. Not infrequently, landlords evicted her for non-

payment of rent, retaining her worldly goods until she came up with the money.

Not to worry. I got over her wayward ways a long time ago by realizing that, though naturally high-spirited ("They call me Spitfire, kid!" she'd say), she fought chronic depression with alcohol, promiscuity, and all the good times she could get. My mother's life had been marked by "indigence" in more ways than one. She died suddenly of them all at fifty-three—broke, in bed, on welfare, all by herself in a room in a public housing project.

In any case, at the end of our rare weekend visits—anxious to get back to her life as a woman on the make—she would dress us up, put us on a train bound for the short trip to Racine, give us a few bucks for cab fare, and bid us tearful farewells in the train car. These were hard moments for us three. We'd tear-up, and she'd wipe her lipsticked kisses from our faces with a damp hankie. "Keep your chins up!" she'd say. Then it was Choo! Choo! and off we'd go—chins up.

It's amusing now to imagine what a cab driver might have thought when Alice and I got off the train, walked up to his taxi like Munchkins on Dress-up Day at the studio, and requested a ride to Taylor Home.

What could have meandered in his mind after he'd dropped us off at the front door of Taylor Home's Victorian edifice, got handed a small wad of cash (including a tip) and then watched two flesh and blood figurines vanish into a brick labyrinth? "Geez!" he might have said, shoving his hat back and scratching his head. "Orphan kids have it a helluva lot better than I thought!" ◉

Imagine what a cab driver might have thought when Alice and
I got off the train, walked up to him like Munchkins on Dress-up Day
at the studio, and requested a ride to Taylor Home.

THE "S" WORD

In which I discover that "stigma" is a noxious weed.

To be stigmatized is to be marginalized. Outside the perimeter of the Home, I often felt that way. Don't get me wrong. I never expected the world to treat me as one of those Hollywood "angels with dirty faces." A garden-variety "dirt-faced kid" would have been just fine with me.

Whenever I harbored feelings akin to lowliness (as I often did), the blame could in no way be traced to the people with whom I lived. While within the Home, whatever stigma I felt inside me I had carried in, like a smelly coat, from the outside world. The Home's air had been cleansed of stigma. There we breathed the oxygen of great expectations.

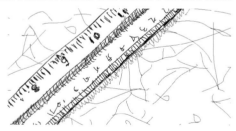

Whether we came from poverty or broken homes or unstable parents or no parents at all, I do not recall the S-word taking root among us. In a sense, once we entered, we belonged. Our footing was equal.

But life outside the Home could be a different story. If "they" knew you were a kid from the Home, you risked being tattooed as one. You feared that the "unsavory" circumstances that had displaced you from a normal home such as "theirs" had disfigured you. "It"—that is, your "plight"—was all your fault.

Or, on another tack, because your parents had failed so miserably, you feared you would inevitably fail, too. Your bloodline was contaminated. Hopes, you believed, were not high for you because of your situation.

When we were teenagers, my sister once put to me that "we have 'the' inferiority complex." She was right. Now and then reoccurrences of what Alice had diagnosed still break out within me, like poison ivy. Stigma is a noxious weed.

Two personal examples of the weed's workings come to mind. Once, a small group of us stopped into a small Taylor Avenue supermarket located on the route home from school. We wandered the store's corridors, not buying anything because, well, we didn't have any money.

Suddenly, we found ourselves confronted by the owner, who apparently knew we were from the Home (we walked in tiny groups past his big circular store window every school day).

He wanted to know what we were up to. He accused us of being the thieves responsible for something gone missing from his shelves on another day. We weren't. We denied stealing from him. He didn't believe us. The scene still sticks with me because of the injustice of it. We were innocent.

After the owner released us, we learned he had called the Home with his allegations. Nothing came of it. The Home believed us. They understood, I suspect, that we had been found guilty by stigma. In a way, however, he had won. We never entered his store again.

Another example—this one of how stigma ebbs and flows according to changing personal circumstances—occurred after my transfer from Mitchell Elementary School to Knapp Elementary in my grandmother's West Racine school district.

....

In the grip of "Mrs. X" I became the recipient of ruler raps on the fingers. I felt like the class whipping boy.

....

During one of my years at Mitchell, in the grip of a Mrs. X, I became the recipient of ruler-raps on the fingers, demeaning comments in front of my classmates, written reprimands, and, in between, pointed indifference. I felt like the class whipping boy.

When, however, I entered Knapp School as a sixth-grader, it was as though the whole of my world had changed over the summer. To my astonishment I was being asked to read aloud, assigned to a crossing guard's position, chosen first for playground team sports.

Never did I second-guess my good fortune. Serendipity spoils under close scrutiny. I simply basked in my new life as the new me at Knapp. Years later though, I did ponder the dynamics of what had happened.

What had happened, I am convinced, is that no one at my new school knew that I was a "kid from the Home." My new Knapp classmates and teacher assumed that I lived in an ordinary neighborhood with two respectable human beings·

of respectable means. That's all. To them I appeared to be a child with, if not great expectations, than at least normal ones. I was the same person, but not from the same "home."

My belittling by Mitchell School's Mrs. X still stings. But life isn't always fair to anyone, and stigma doesn't make it any fairer. Besides, Mrs. X had to live, day-in-day-out, from inside out, with Mrs. X. Now that's what I call fair. ◉

LIFE'S YOUR SANDBOX

*In which I sum up Miss Crossfield's
principles of jumpin' for joy.*

M*iss Crossfield.* How's that for a name novelist Charles Dickens would have loved? Our Miss Crossfield, however, was not a fictional character.

Taylor Home's Grace Crossfield tirelessly directed children's "activities" during my six years there. Though she kept us busy during scheduled activities—even absorbed—she trusted us with our free time.

If she had carried a business card, rest assured that "Idle Hands Are the Devil's Tools" would not have been imprinted on it. Miss Crossfield believed that idle hours are the tools of these words beginning with the prefix *in: inspiration, introspection, independence.* (And incidentally, had she lived and worked during the present era, I'm certain the word *internet* would not have made the list.)

These core convictions put Miss Crossfield perfectly in line with one of Taylor Children's Home's essential philosophies: that the Home's children find ample amounts of both time and liberty on their hands. In a mission statement written years before my time at the Home, a superintendent had this to say:

Had it been inscribed above every door, the unwritten credo of the Home would have gone like this: LIFE'S A LESSON. LIFE'S YOUR SANDBOX. LIFE'S A CLIMB UP THE TARZAN TREE.

We try at every point to make our Home as informal as we
can with a great deal of freedom... We are in the business...
to develop happy children, well-adjusted children, inde-
pendent children who can think for themselves... who can
create... and like to use their imaginations.

No time-frantic soccer moms and hockey dads for us kids at the Home! No supervised homework by the clock or math tutors following dinner. And no, absolutely no, SUV rides to after-school polo, yoga or fencing lessons.

Instead, during our idle hours we played with the hours as if they consisted of unopened canisters of Play Dough, Froebel blocks or Tinker Toys. With these toys, "lost" time meant time to find ourselves through unsupervised play as individuals. The same applied to spontaneous group play. Outdoor games of, for instance, "Kick the Can" hinged on *our* initiative, including finding a suitable can.

Put simply, Taylor Children's Home trusted each of us to choose what was best for us, even if some of those choices went bad like reducing Bird's Jungle to scorched earth (see "Fire in the Jungle") or secretly peering down an attic ventilation grate to watch a bedtime parade of girls in pink Snuggies.

"We believe," the same superintendent had written, "that the climate of the Home must be free enough that a child can break rules and get into difficulty without feeling as if the sky will fall in on him."

In other words, the unwritten credo of Taylor Home, had it been inscribed above every door, would have been taken from a list like this one:

Life's a lesson.
Life's your sandbox.
Life's a climb up the Tarzan Tree.

(Miss Crossfield, rest assured, would have insisted that you were free to choose one or some or none at all.) ❁

FIRE IN THE JUNGLE

In which I outrun a runaway grass fire but can't outrun the consequences.

We called our personal piece of wilderness "Bird's Jungle," although it belonged to some private, probably absentee, landowner. Taylor Home back then sat on the edge of city, the entryway to largely undeveloped countryside between Racine and Kenosha.

Bird's Jungle lay on the other side of Taylor Avenue, a short tramp over an open field to a low-lying area of woodland entangled with tall shrubs. In those days we wouldn't have known what to make of a "No Trespassing" sign if we'd  seen one. Rural properties were less "posted" then. Thus, "Bird's Jungle" became a free-reign, *sanctum sanctorum* for a few of us during vacant hours.

Summertime "interlopers" may have penetrated our wilderness retreat, but we never saw signs of them. And if they had, they could be forgiven for thinking they'd stumbled upon a tiny, freshly abandoned Native American village. Empty green lean-tos, constructed with latticed tree limbs and snugly woven leafy branches would have had them rubbing their eyes.

Two weeks spent every July at the YMCA's Camp Anokijig (an-oh-kee-gee) had taught us well. We knew our Indian woodcraft. Each summer the Home's staff took a breather by booking us for two weeks at Camp Anokijig near Elkhart Lake in one of Wisconsin's beauti-

One gray march afternoon, our Camp Anokijig training failed us.
More likely, we failed our trainers.

ful kettle moraine areas. My five-year, moth-eaten, flannel Anokijig camper badge remains one of my most prized possessions.

A verse from the camp's signature song, as I recall, went something like this:

> *Anokijig,*
> *Where the campers*
> *Play like Indians,*
> *Building campfires*
> *At their doors.*

After a stint at camp, why wouldn't "playing like Indians" be in our blood? Sung to the melody of a Sousa march, the camp's anthem ended with this rousing chorus:

> *Anokijig,*
> *May we ever*
> *Praise thy Name!*

I still praise its name and, I'm sure, so do many others. It still exists, although no longer funded by the YMCA.

One gray March afternoon, however, our camp training failed us. More likely, we failed our trainers. The incident began on a chilly, early spring Saturday. Looking for something to do, a small group of us week-end boys, decided to trek to Bird's Jungle. Because the leaves weren't out yet, there'd have been no rebuilding of last year's huts. Instead, a new idea struck us: We'd have, *a la* Camp Anokijig, a woodland cookout over a campfire!

> *Anokijig,*
> *We'll fry bacon*
> *In thy name.*

We had a plan. First step: Go to the cooks in the Home's kitchen with our idea. Second step: Talk the cooks into giving us some eggs and bacon. Third: Ask for a frying pan. Fourth: Head for Bird's Jungle with some matches. Fifth: Head out fast, before the cooks change their minds.

So off we went to Bird's Jungle with a fry pan, a few eggs ("no bacon, boys") and matches. In no time we sat around a crackling campfire watching raw eggs curl white in the pan, while, for all I know, singing camp songs like this one:

> *Camp Anokijig, boys!*
> *That's where there's more,*
> *That's where there's horseback riding*
> *And there's boats that line the shor-or.*

Suddenly one of us yelled, "Fire!!!" We sprang to our feet. Sure enough, the floor of the woods smoldered among licks of flame. What to do?!? Boy, are we in for it! We jerked off our coats and began beating the flames. Damn! The flames wouldn't be cowed. The fire was spreading. What now?!? One of us, we decided, must run back to the Home to have someone call the Fire Department! Me! Why me?

I found myself running hard toward the Home, wondering what might await me when I told them we'd set Bird's Jungle on fire. Our missing bacon would be fried, for sure.

I bolted through the front door, stopped a supervisor and gasped the news. But as she reached for the phone, I pivoted, speeding headlong out the same front door, bent on rejoining my friends at the flaming scene of the crime.

Tried and true members of the Racine City Fire Department, wearing black fire-fighter's hats, arrived in short order, leaped from their siren-red truck, took a quick, sober glance at the situation, and then began subduing the flames with brooms. Straw brooms! In no time, these guys had methodically and nonchalantly quelled the blaze by sweeping it to smokeless cinders.

As I recall, no one in this squad of Racine's finest reprimanded us. More likely, their grins bid us a farewell as, without an escort, we marched ourselves back to the Home to take our medicine. The medicine? Sixty minutes sitting silently—and sheepishly—in tall-back chairs, our feet dangling like those of hanged convicts. The worst, however, awaited me on the blackened floor of Bird's Jungle.

In the dash to the Home for help, I'd abandoned to the fire a brand new spring coat my grandmother had given me. It had suffered irreparable damage. No longer brown but ashen, once resplendent now raggedy, I carried it back to the Home as if it were a limp, elfin corpse.

But the news turned to good news in the end: My smoldering coat appeared to be the only casualty of the incident, except for the pride of the coat's owner, who, like a noble native of Anokijig, asked his grandmother for forgiveness. Hallelujah! She immediately forgave me. "Anokijig, May We Ever Praise Thy Name!" ❂

CANDY BAR CHRISTIANS

In which an evangelist husband and wife "bar"
their basement door with chocolate.

Taylor Children's Home treated organized religion as a matter of choice. My choice was Clark Bars. ("Real Milk Chocolate. Real Peanut Butter Crunch.")

While supervisors did lead us in a short recited prayer before meals, that was pretty much it for religious practices at the Home. Early in its history as Taylor Orphan Asylum, the chapel had often been used for services. The room's dark-stained wood pews, ministerial lectern, stained glass windows, vaulted ceiling, and tiny ornate organ spoke volumes of the room's spiritual character. But times had changed, and except for the rare special event, the chapel doors remained closed to us.

Christianity pretty much shaped the culture of Taylor Orphan Asylum— far more, however, as an underlying philosophy of care than as a doctrine. Simply put, "Do unto others as you would want them to do unto you" kept the Home's hearth fires burning for us.

As a result, if we children participated in organized religious activities, they tended to occur outside the Home. I can recall, for instance, attending Catholic services with my grandparents in West

For Quick Energy!

CLARK

I remember Bible lessons in the basement of a couple's private home.
I confess Clark Bars lured me there.

Racine on some Sundays while other Sabbath days were spent at Protestant Sunday School sessions with a few other kids at a church on Taylor Avenue.

Most of all, however, I remember voluntarily attending a once a-week, after-school Bible lesson in the basement of a couple's private home near Mitchell School. I confess that Clark Bars lured me there.

Apparently, these two had an Evangelical bent that called them to sponsor short Good Book tutorials for kids in their home. When the day came each week, their basement room filled with eager child-acolytes, salivating, the couple thought, for Christ.

The "stage" for their message consisted of a green flannel board positioned on a tripod at the front of the room. Paper cutouts of Biblically significant figures and shapes lay in wait in a box next to the board.

As the lesson proceeded, if one or the other mentioned a shepherd and his flock, a sheep-keeper holding a crook and some white, wooly sheep would be stuck onto the flannel. If a manger were mentioned, a stable, donkey and ancient humans in robes and sandals would be pressed to the green. The scenarios proved as bounteous as the Bible itself.

They talked on and on. And on and on. Although our hosts were indubitably of goodwill, their talking ate up goodly amounts of time, made even more maddening by our unholy hunger for the sacred Clark Bars. Nevertheless, we held our chairs. No one—absolutely no one—fled the room early. The grand, mouth-watering finale awaited us. Amen.

At lesson's end, the couple would stroll to the rear of the room, remove a fresh carton of two-dozen bars from a cabinet and then move to the door as though transporting the Holy Grail. The exit ceremony, however, required that we continue to keep our chairs. Our self-restraint thickened the air we breathed. "One row at a time, single-file, boys and girls, starting this time with the last row, please,"

As we passed in a feverish line through the door, we each, at long last, seized upon the prize we had suffered so mightily for. We tore up the stairs into the street, leaving wrappers in our wake.

Believe me, if I ever again spot a sheep on a flannel board, I'll drool for a Clark Bar. ○

NEXT DOOR MAGI

In which Christmas comes wrapped in community charity.

Shed your tears into the punch bowl, stash your sympathy in a Yule stocking and take down the black tinsel on the tree for us. The Christmas season was festive for us kids at the Home. Plenty of joyous consolations—call them fringe benefits—piled up for us during the holidays.

Throughout the period local "Magi" (philanthropists, including members of the Home's board of directors) would pitch in to buy us presents. Their gifts would be distributed during a pre-Christmas ceremony attended by donors, many in suits and furs, gathered in the Home's chapel.

The chapel doors opened only on this occasion, as I recall. That, of course, added to the magic. I remember singularly beautiful evenings spent there during those Christmases.

A giant, spiraling fir tree was erected, the chapel's small ornate organ tuned-up, and carols rehearsed for singing with visiting strangers that night. We felt genuinely exhilarated—grateful, I'll dare to say, even if the next day we came up empty-handed after searching the empty pews for loose change.

One Christmas my sister and I actually got to go home for the holidays with a married couple who I suspect served on Taylor Home's board of directors. Alice and I had nowhere to go for Christmas, so these two had offered the season's comforts of their lavish life to us. Philanthropy, as I learned, can begin at home. I recall hoping this couple would adopt us. They didn't, but even if they had hoped to declare us their own, it would not have been possible. Our mother's legal custody of us was absolute, and she absolutely hung on to it. We were, in a way, her only possessions.

Throughout the holidays there were other displays of charity from the community. Racine at that time was a thriving industrial city—a good place to get a good job at a fair wage.

A tradition in some of the factories was the employee Christmas party. The Home's charges were often invited. That meant more candy, more toys, more gleefulness. Hurray for Johnson Wax! Bravo for J.I. Case! Three cheers for a holiday handful of Horlicks' malted milk balls.

Perhaps nothing as touching, however, occurred during Taylor Home's spell of Christmas than what took place in the small neighborhood to the immediate south of the Home. There, by tradition on a designated December day, small bags of fruit and other Christmas snacks would be handed to us from the front doors.

These houses were not the residences of the wealthy, the estates of industrialists, the lake-view penthouses of the fantastically prosperous. They were the habitations of ordinary people of ordinary means from which the ordinary smell of home cooking ushered as they unlatched their front doors.

We knocked. They opened. "Happy holidays!" We were their neighbors. "Next door" meant open doors to us at Christmas, when stigma took a holiday. ⊙

We knocked. They opened. "Happy holidays!" Next door meant
open doors to us at Christmas, when stigma took a holiday.

QUARANTINED

In which poliomyelitis erases a classmate's life.

M y years at the Home coincided with some of the great polio scares of the era. To forestall outbreaks of the highly infectious disease, Racine imposed citywide quarantines of children in their homes, especially, as I recall, during the summer. Until the advent of the Salk vaccine in the '50s, the fear of infantile paralysis spooked our childhoods along with Bela Lugosi, Hollywood's consummate bogeyman.

Children at the Home were considered at greater risk than children in single-family homes. The more kids congregated in one place, the greater the danger of infection. Nonetheless, I recollect no child in the care of Taylor Home contracting polio during my years there.

Imaginary symptoms, however, rampaged through the Home, though most of us suffered our fears silently. Stiff necks, muscle pains, headaches, fevers, bad dreams—all ordinary assaults on the human condition—became the threat of a life sentence in an iron lung, imprisoned and immovable with nothing to stare at but our own stare in a mirror.

Ironically, during the quarantines those of us at the Home had it much better than kids down the block. We had each other, the run of our gigantic "mansion" on several acres, and cheerful adult attendants to keep us happy and homey.

Other kids, however, usually had only a brother or a sister, two parents, maybe a two-bedroom Cape Cod and a tiny backyard to amuse themselves within. A friend of my age, raised alone during the day at home in West Allis, Wisconsin (his parents both worked), relates this story: Quarantines got so boring that he invented a game for himself. He'd sneak out the door, dash down the street to a stop sign, touch it, spin around, and then speed back to his house. By his own rules, if he hadn't experienced polio symptoms by morning, he'd won the "game."

Some children, however, didn't "win the game." I learned that melancholy fact firsthand in September of 1948, during a brief, abortive, placement with my maternal grandmother and step-grandfather in West Racine.

The move to my grandparent's house necessitated that I switch from south Racine's Mitchell Elementary School to West Racine's Gilbert Knapp Elementary. Within a few weeks, a boy enrolled in my sixth-grade classroom died—actually *died*—of polio.

The school, of course, went into shock, accompanied by deliberations with health officials. The upshot was that my sixth-grade classmates and I were offered two-week "home quarantines": Not a bad life for a kid who loved his grandparents, "Mabel" and "Bernie."

They doted on me, and I returned the favor by savoring my new life as the "only child" in a household as comfortably respectable as a movie set's version of life in America. On the other hand, my sister, Alice, although she remained in her rural foster home seemed as happy as the clucking, snow-white chickens she got to throw corn kernels to.

However, these sunny developments for each of us marked an unexpected turning point in our lives. By the end of my two-week quarantine, Alice and I found ourselves living with our mother in a one-

....

He'd sneak out the door, dash down the street to a stop sign, touch it and then speed back to his house. By his own rules, if hadn't experienced polio symptoms by morning, he'd won the "game."

....

room basement apartment in Milwaukee's inner city, enrolled in yet another school. Life had sucker-punched us again.

My dark experience of a classmate's death by polio didn't faze me for long. Another category of illness now seized my attention. (See "A Street Car Named Delirium" and its sequel "Punch Drunk.")

A STREETCAR
NAMED DELIRIUM

A Three-Scene Script for a Three-Minute Movie

In which I make an off-my-trolley dash for freedom only to be captured by a cab.

Scene One

November 1948. A weekday. A boy (age 11), a girl (age 9), and their mother (age 31) sit on a streetcar grinding along a busy Milwaukee street. Clang-clang. Clang-clang. The children are dressed for school, the mother, though some-what disheveled, is dressed fashionably, albeit cheaply, as if on a downtown shop-ping excursion. The boy sits in the seat directly in front of his sister and 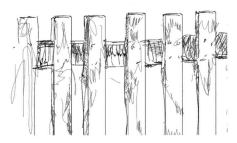 mother, who are sitting together across from the rear, right-side exit door.

Action

The streetcar squeaks to a halt, letting passengers enter and disembark. Quickly, the boy jumps up and dashes out the open rear door to the sidewalk. The mother spots him. "David!" She stands up hurriedly, grabbing her daughter by the hand and yanking her toward the closing door. The streetcar begins to move. "Stop!" she screams at the driver. "Stop! That's my son! Open the door!" The streetcar jerks to a halt, the doors open, and the mother exits, gripping her daughter by the shoulders. "David!" she shouts. "What are you doing? Come back, David!" The boy turns and runs down a side street.

Scene Two

Seconds later. A taxi cruises the area. The driver spots a woman and little girl at a streetcar stop.

Action

The women yells, "Taxi! Taxi!" It stops. She opens the rear door, pulling the girl into the backseat. "Follow that boy! That one!" [pointing down the street, where the boy has halted to look back]. "He's my son! A runaway!" The driver flips the flag on the meter. "Whatever you say, lady. Relax."

The taxi turns and heads down the street toward the boy. The boy again breaks into a run. The vehicle pursues him cautiously. The boy is now dashing across lawns, jumping fences, sprinting up alleys and down leafless residential streets. The taxi continues to shadow him. Abruptly the boy stops on a sidewalk, stooped, hands on his knees and out of breath. The taxi pulls up alongside. The boy lifts his head toward his mother as she scrambles out the rear door. He's sobbing. She jerks him into the taxi. "To the hospital! Take us to the hospital! This boy's gone crazy!"

Scene Three

Thirty minutes later. The mother sits with a nurse in a hospital consultation room, empty except for them. The nurse is carefully examining the mother's left hand. The mother is distraught, eyes closed, head rocking back and forth. Her feet tap in nervous unison. A physician wearing a white coat enters, closing the door quietly behind him.

"Follow that boy! He's my son! He's a runaway!" The taxi driver flips
the flag on the meter. *"Whatever you say, lady. Relax."*

Action

"Mrs. Rozelle," says the physician, "I've now had separate talks with your children and, as you know, with you. How are you doing?" The mother looks up, wild-eyed, "That boy! That boy! What got into him? I can't take it anymore!" The physician nods as if to sympathize.

"Mrs. Rozelle, we think it best if you and your children had a rest from each other. Times have been very hard for the three of you." She breaks into tears. "In addition, it appears that your hand is badly infected." "Yes, I cut it at work," she sobs. He nods. "I've just contacted the Children's Service Society so that David and Alice can be returned to—let's see here [glancing at his clipboard]—Taylor Children's Home in Racine for the time being."

The mother trembles. "But what about me, doctor? What am I going to do? I'm afraid! I need my children with me." He places his hand gently on her shoulder. "Mrs. Rozelle, a stay in the hospital would be best for you. You won't be alone there. Your children will be fine."

....

Epilogue

My sister and I re-entered Taylor Home that afternoon. Within a few days, Alice had rejoined her foster parents in rural Racine County. As for me, I settled back into the life of the Home, though gnawed by guilt for what I believed my failed escape attempt had brought down upon my mother.

Thanks to the swift intervention of the Wisconsin Children's Service Society, my sister and I had been rescued from a deeply troubled life in our mother's custody. In lockstep with her breakdown, our wobbly, three-legged life as a "family" had broken. Within days we had been returned to the protective custody of kindly, caring "strangers" while our penniless mother had been hospitalized for treatment of her injuries, both physical and mental. Is it any wonder that I grew to adulthood with a matter-of-fact confidence in my government's "safety net"? It had, after all, underwritten my dreams of a better life and rescued my mother—for the rest of her life—from unremitting wretchedness.

On that frenzied November day in 1948, Alice and I had been plucked from a life of wandering city streets day after day with a parent who, day by day, sank ever deeper into mental illness. She had held us from school for days on end, too terrified to be alone, too ill to be responsible, too disturbed to be rational. She could no longer muster either the courage or the means to be a mother to us. Alice and I had, for two months, become the child caretakers of a mother gone mad. Taylor Home had saved us again. ✹

PUNCH DRUNK

*In which my troubled state of mind makes
for trouble in a classroom.*

Events during the autumn of 1948 left me psychologically punch drunk—pounded onto the ropes of my eleven-year-old life. I had ventured out of Taylor Home and into the world out there only to return by first snowfall, emotionally clobbered.

Late that summer my mother had agreed, at last, to my placement with my grandmother and her second husband in West Racine. I had no objection. I loved my Grandma Mabel and Grandpa Bernie. I loved Racine, since 1944 my "hometown," dimly aware that it can take a city that felt like a village to raise a child.

September in West Racine flew by merrily for me. I'd been welcome—even cherished—at 3315 Victory Avenue, my grandparent's home. And to my astonishment my new school, Knapp Elementary, had sweetened my sense of self-worth. No one at Knapp knew or much less cared that I had lived at Taylor Home. My ego and I excelled both in school and at home.

By the first of October, however, my mother had struck again. Unable to contain her volcanic animosity toward her mother (my grandmother), she demanded that my sister and I be relocated to live with her

in central Milwaukee. The legal system had complied. Because of her status in law as sole custodial parent, her wish had become the law's command.

Our new home in Milwaukee—White Row Apartments, 935 13th Street—consisted of a single basement room flanking an alley. Our small, locked kitchen lay at the end of the basement corridor. Our bathroom (a sink, a stool and a shower) occupied a small, unlocked room in the building's laundry room.

Our mother worked nights as a waitress at a restaurant downtown. Her tips barely paid the rent, when she paid it. We lived close to the bone, and eventually there was no bone.

In short order our mother had experienced what I now recognize as a severe mental breakdown and jettisoned her job, leaving us on short rations. One day she had sent me to a local grocery store to buy a chicken for us on credit. My boy's face didn't sway the grocer. He refused. "Sorry, kid. Your mom's tab is too big."

Worse than that she had begun suffering attacks of full-blown anxiety. These left her too terrified to be alone for a moment let alone an entire school day. As a result, we became our mother's round-the-clock companions, out of school with an out-of-her-mind mom. Day by day, hand in hand we wandered Milwaukee's streets. Night by night we locked ourselves in our basement room. We had become each other's captives.

By November, however, the inevitable hell had broken loose (see "A Street Car Named Delirium"). Consequently, Milwaukee Children's Service Society—thanks to a tip from Taylor Home—had swooped in to return us to sane and safe surroundings: Alice to her foster home in the country, David to his Taylor Home. Oh, happy day, sort of.

....

I stood up in a panic, slammed my palms to my ears and screamed,
"I can't hear! I can't hear!" The classroom went silent.

....

Not so happy for me, however, back at Racine Mitchell School, where my old classmates and our new sixth grade teacher were in for a psychiatric melodrama. My intellect had deteriorated like plaster from a sodden ceiling. I couldn't even remember how to do multiplication and long division. I simply could not subdue the chaos that roiled and boiled inside me.

In the classroom one day, I did something that brought matters to a climactic boil. As I sat at my desk, the turmoil inside my head became unbearable. I stood up in a panic, slammed my palms to my ears and screamed, "I can't hear! I can't hear!" The room went silent. "I can't hear!" The teacher sped to my side. Excited chatter followed me out the door in her grip.

Needless to say, I didn't need an audiologist. I needed a psychologist. And so Mitchell School in 1948 did the best it could for my classmates and me. I spent the balance of that school year in a classroom reserved for marginally developmentally disabled students.

The switch in classrooms did not, however, **add** to my angst. It **subtracted** from it. The change proved to be therapeutic. The kindliness of my new teacher, in harmony with the amiability of my new classmates, won the days left for me in sixth grade. As far as I can remember, any "stigma" attached to my outburst never landed a glove on me. I began to feel whole again.

As a matter of fact, during the months I took refuge in that classroom, something singularly gratifying happened to me—something that had never happened before in all my years at Mitchell Elementary. A classmate actually showed interest in where and how I lived. "What's it like where you live?" "Do you have your own room?" "Do you eat with the other kids?" "Can I go with you for a visit?"

And so it came to pass that I gave this boy a personal tour of my home. As I recall, he was fascinated, maybe even a little envious. Could it be that the grass on my side of the fence looked greener to him?

Whatever he may have thought, by having the courage to be curious, this one guileless classmate who came from beyond the fence lines of the Home, had given me my one chance to show pride in where I lived. *Mmmmm-ann-gann-niii!* (See "The Tarzan Tree.") ◉

AN OFFER I COULDN'T REFUSE

In which Miss Roskilly trusts me to pick a foster home.

Mission statements are a dime a dozen. The director of a public human services agency I once worked for dismissed them as "wall hangings." Asked to describe the guiding principles of his organization, his replies amounted to third-rate song-and-dance routines. He could have saved his lungs and legs by just pointing to a wall.

To my knowledge, Taylor Children's Home never sang and danced its mission away. During my six years there, it lived its founding principles. Medora Roskilly, the Home's superintendent, would have no more tolerated institutional hypocrisy than assented to putting a difficult child on bread and water.

Three personal proofs of Taylor Home's fealty to mission come to mind. Each, in my opinion, demonstrates not only its adherence to the letter of its principles, but a willingness to reach beyond them. Going "beyond the call of duty" seemed to come as naturally to its caregivers as ivy to its outer walls.

In 1944 I had been admitted to the Home following a physical examination that declared me markedly underweight. The Home's response? Not just regular servings of regular meals at regular nutritional values. Cream got poured on my cereal. Butter became my buddy. I'm surprised I didn't find Wisconsin cheddar stashed under my pillow.

Here's more evidence of the Home's commitment to its principles: In 1948, following Alice's and my ill-fated return to our mother's care, Taylor Children's Home—although not legally obligated to do so—kept its ear to the ground about our welfare in Milwaukee. Their concern proved prescient. Our well-being had indeed deteriorated (see "A Streetcar Named Delirium" and "Punch Drunk").

Alarmed by what it had heard, the Home's supervising social worker, Mildred Wright, dispatched a letter to Milwaukee's Children's Service Society inquiring about our situation. "Have you heard anything about the Rozelle children?" the letter asked. "We have heard they have fallen on hard times." How's that for a public institution giving a damn about children it no longer had a vested interest in, except as a matter of conscience?

And finally this third proof of the Home's extraordinary adherence to mission: by June of 1949, I was, at eleven years old, fast approaching the age when the Home had been directed to seek foster care for its oldest children. Throughout that summer, the Home's superintendent, Medora Roskilly, and I engaged in a number of informal chats in her office about my impending placement in a foster home. Remarkably, she had no intention of relocating me anywhere unless she had my consent to do so.

One day she described for me in some detail her first offering of a foster home and then invited me to spend a little time thinking about it before deciding. I did. When I returned, I told her that I preferred

I had become a "foster kid." My worldly goods that day included a tattered biography of Babe Ruth. In it I had listed the names of the friends I'd left behind at Taylor Home.

not to go there. Her response? As I recall, she calmly accepted my decision in spite of the fact that foster homes were as hard to find in 1949 as they are in 2013. The pressure upon her to relocate me surely continued.

Perhaps my old "coyote" instincts (see "Hell Hole Sundays") had warned me I wouldn't be happy in the home she'd first proposed. Or maybe I just wasn't "ready" to leave. In any case, Miss Roskilly, in deferring to me, had acted in concert with the Home's mission to shape "independent children, who can think for themselves." On that day, Taylor Orphan Asylum's founding spirits—Isaac and Emmerline Taylor—may have smiled down upon Medora Roskilly and me.

Later that summer, though, she made me an offer I couldn't refuse. My sister had been placed months before with foster parents among dairy farmers in Racine County. Alice had found a measure of happiness at last, and she wanted me, her brother, to share in it. She had a point. She and I, we had learned, were the only immediate family we could entrust with our welfare.

Our father, whom we had not seen in a decade, had retreated to Wisconsin's North Woods long ago. Our perennially warring mother and grandmother had made their homes no-fly zones for us. Given the inevitability of my separation from the Home, I gave in. I told Miss Roskilly that I would join my sister.

On September 1, 1949, after nearly six years at home at Taylor Children's Home, I began a new life among strangers. Instead of a "kid from the Home," I had become "a foster kid." My worldly goods that day included a tattered biography of Babe Ruth. In it I had listed the names of the friends I'd left behind at Taylor Home.

My foster mother reported to the Home that I cried that first night. Who wouldn't? I'd lost my home. ✹

POSTSCRIPT ON
A VALENTINE

In which on her deathbed, Medora Roskilly
makes room to see me "Home."

My separation from the Home at age twelve turned out to be final. But it was *final* only insofar as I never lived again under the roof of Isaac and Emmerline Taylor. I have, nonetheless, never stopped, in the broadest sense of the word, *living* at 3211 Taylor Avenue, Racine, Wisconsin.

The evidence resides in me, a grateful witness, and in this memoir, a makeshift "memorial."

There also exists evidence that I had not been forgotten there after my departure—a fact unquestionably true for hundreds of other children who had called Taylor Home their home. In my case, the proof remains in my hands: a yellowing newspaper clipping dated 1957, and a fading Valentine's Day card dated 1952. Let's begin with 1957, and then move five years backward to 1952.

1957

By the mid-fifties I had entered college, taking to student life like a coyote to a lamb chop. I possessed almost nothing material. On the other hand, I needed almost nothing material. My university days still represent the most luxurious years of my life. I'd learned my lessons well at Taylor Home: luxury is less and less is more.

In my sophomore year I had been named to an editor's post on the college newspaper. I liked to write, and my assignments for *The Royal Purple* actually got me into print.

Now, jump ahead thirty years later, to the early '80s, when I sifted through Taylor Children's Home archives for records of my history as "a kid from the Home." Unexpectedly, I found plenty in a thick file folder under my name. Because the time I'd set aside was short, I hurried through the pages.

One document, however, stopped me in my tracks. It was a clipping of a 1957 press release that had appeared in *The Racine Journal Times*. There I was! My picture looked out at me from a short article that announced I'd been named an editor of my college newspaper. I was

....

Miss Crossfield replied, "Dear David, It was nice to get your letter.
I got it the day Miss Roskilly died and read it to her hours
before she died."

....

mystified. I still am. Who had clipped this? Who had placed an inconsequential press release in a file "closed" nearly twenty years before? And why?

1952

In early 1952, more than two years after departing Taylor Home I had written a letter from my foster home addressed to Miss Crossfield. My purpose had been to find the address of one of my friends. She replied by mail with a personal note on a Valentine's Day card to my sister and me.

I still have it, one of those tiny, thin paper, penny cards with a child-like, "heartfelt" message on the front. Purchased in packs, they were commonly exchanged in those days as a way of saying, as hers did, "It's easy as ABC to like you."

But more importantly, on the back Miss Crossfield had handwritten in blue ink a short message which begins this way:

> *Dear David, It was nice to get your letter. I got it the day Miss Roskilly died and read it to her hours before she died.*

Medora Roskilly had served in a long, distinguished line of Taylor Orphan Asylum superintendents—a keeper of the covenant set forth in the will of Isaac and Emmerline Taylor. In that role she had served as not only chief caretaker of those of us entrusted to the Home, but also as our champion.

On her deathbed in 1952, Medora Roskilly had listened to her colleague Grace Crossfield read my letter. Do I fool myself when I say that Miss Roskilly, in her dying thoughts, made way for a child from Taylor Home? I think not. ◉

ACKNOWLEDGEMENTS

*The only things that are important in
life are the things you remember.*

—Jean Renoir

Books, like memories, are "made" not born.
Heartfelt thanks to my precious wife Judith Reith-Rozelle
and good friend Christian Andrew Grooms for their vital
roles in the "making" of *The Kid Who
Climbed the Tarzan Tree.*

And for their varied participation in this memoir's realization,
I have also abundant reason to remember Bob Albrightson,
Bette and Tom Grover, Eric Hanson, Julie Tallard Johnson,
Donn and Laurie Lind, Kristin Mitchell of Little Creek Press,
Albert Pitts, Carl Stratman, the Racine Heritage Museum,
Taylor Children's Home, the Waterford Public Library,
the Wisconsin Historical Society and
Hanshan Wright-Miller.

—D.W. Rozelle

ABOUT THE AUTHOR

David William Rozelle lives in retirement with his wife Judith, a plant scientist, in Wisconsin's Wyoming Township near Spring Green. Following his boyhood at Taylor Home and in a rural foster home, he earned an undergraduate degree at Wisconsin State College-Whitewater and did graduate work at universities in both Colorado and California.

Author David Rozelle, perhaps age eleven. Photograph believed taken during Rozelle's last summer at Taylor Children's Home, 1949.

Rozelle's accomplishments as a young University of Wisconsin System faculty member won him a Fulbright grant in 1971-72. Posted to Denmark, he taught American literature at five Danish colleges.

Since 1973, his resume has included positions as associate director of an antipoverty agency, community services director of a large rural mental health center, and assignments as freelance writer and creative consultant for a number of public education programs, often in the field of preventive mental health.

A published poet, essayist and former guest political columnist, Rozelle has for years collaborated as "poet in residence" with his distinguished artist friend Christian Andrew Grooms on events for Paoli House Gallery in Wisconsin. Grooms, who is the gallery's artistic director, graciously volunteered to be this book's illustrator.

The Kid Who Climbed the Tarzan Tree represents Rozelle's long-delayed written celebration of his six years as a "kid from the Home." His deepest gratitude goes out to his wife Judith and friend Christian for not only believing in this work but also making it an immeasurably better one. He is honored by their presence in his life and in the book's publication.

ABOUT THE ILLUSTRATOR

Christian Andrew Grooms, born in 1971, currently lives and works in Madison, Wisconsin. After studying for his BFA at the University of Minnesota, Minneapolis/St. Paul, Grooms earned a Master

Artist Christian Andrew Grooms at about six, the age that David Rozelle entered Taylor Children's Home. Family photograph circa 1977.

of Fine Arts degree from Parsons School of Design, New York University, New York, N.Y.

His artwork—which includes illustration, painting, drawing, printmaking, sculpture and audio production—has been exhibited in the Midwest, New York City, Connecticut and in Germany. In addition, he has created artwork for Madison Opera, Roche, Inc. and continues to illustrate for Full Compass Systems. He is also a musician, former sound engineer for Minnesota Public Radio, and has both created and produced record albums, including cover art.

Grooms serves as part owner/founder and artistic director of Paoli House Gallery. Paoli—once the site of an historic gristmill on the Sugar River in Wisconsin's Dane County—has been reincarnated as an arts community. Many of Grooms' creations, along with those of other contemporary artists, can be found on exhibition there.

Grooms asserts that as he sketched illustrations for this work, modeling help from nine-year-old Hanshan Dorje Wright-Miller and his brother Japhy, age 12, enabled him to visualize "the timeless qualities that children of all eras possess." He thanks Hanshan especially for sitting with him for several late hours, watching him draw and assisting him along the way. Hanshan, he confesses, even drew parts of the compositions.

115

ABOUT THE ILLUSTRATOR'S ASSISTANT

Illustrator's Assistant Hanshan Dorje Wright-Miller

My hobbies are bike riding, skate boarding, and being outside.

Hanshan Wright-Miller, age nine, friend/associate of Christian Andrew Grooms. Photograph taken on steps of Paoli House Gallery, 2013.

ARTISTS' AND AUTHOR'S STATEMENTS

Author David William Rozelle

I believe that recollection is the brain's impressionism—fast strokes of sensory impressions given order by containment on a "canvas" whose dimensions are limited by the "memory" itself. Because I am—when all is said and done—a poet, I chose to reconstruct my years at the Home as an "arc" of distilled, loosely chronological "flashbacks," trusting that the whole would surpass the sum of its parts. For that I owe incalculable praise to Andy Grooms, who offered to confirm the book's concept by reading each vignette quickly and then sketching whatever flew into his imagination. It worked. His "mind sketches" have pushed my memoir beyond the "arc" of my conception. What is more, our collaboration has pushed my joy in writing beyond boundaries held too close for too long.

....

Illustrator Christian Andrew Grooms

I was honored when Dave asked me to illustrate this book. Or, was it my own enthusiasm selfishly volunteering my services? It was probably the latter, considering that I have become quite an admirer of his writing over the last six years of our friendship. Dave's writing evokes strong imagery that covers a very dynamic range of emotions. With that said, my plan of attack was to draw as I read and to document the visual journey as it came to me chronologically. My goal was to assist future readers' imaginations and offer up this first reader's first impressions of these wonderful memoirs. But most of all, thanks to Dave for inviting me into his story and allowing me to participate in one of the most meaningful collaborations I have ever experienced.

....

Illustrator's Assistant Hanshan Dorje Wright-Miller

I like drawing. You have to be relaxed and it takes a lot of practice. It's like you can do anything with a pencil and some paper.

THE END

It's 1944.

A little boy and his sister find themselves the
wards of strangers in a cavernous children's home.
Their mother assures them that their stay will be but a
few months. Nearly six years later what they thought was
to be a "stay" ends with their placement in a foster home.
While this sounds like a chapter written by Charles
Dickens in one of his darker moods, it isn't. Looking
back after a half century, that "little boy," D.W. Rozelle,
remembers his years at "the Home" as the best years
of his tumultuous boyhood. Over 25 drawings
by distinguished artist C.A. Grooms lend
Rozelle's flashbacks a startling
visual impact.

$15.95
ISBN 978-0-9896431-5-3

9 780989 643153

www.littlecreekpress.com